MOUTHFUL OF CINDERS

ADESIYAN OLUWAPELUMI

This is a work of fiction. All names, characters, places, and incidents are a product of the author's imagination. Any resemblance to real events or persons, living or dead, is entirely coincidental.

Published by Akashic Books

ISBN: 978-1-63614-251-7

Printed in China
First printing

EU Authorized Representative details:
Easy Access System Europe
Mustamäe tee 50, 10621 Tallinn, Estonia
gpsr.request@easproject.com

Akashic Books
Instagram, X, Facebook: AkashicBooks
info@akashicbooks.com
www.akashicbooks.com

African Poetry Book Fund
Brown University
10 Prospect Street
Box A
Providence, RI 02912

TABLE OF CONTENTS

PREFACE

by Nick Makoha

At times, the mantle of a poet is a heavy burden. Adesiyan Oluwapelumi picks up that burden in his thirteen-poem chapbook, *Mouthful of Cinders*. He is not talking about past events that we can meander through in hindsight while completing the crossword or recapping the day's football scores. His utterance comes directly from situations affecting the people of Nigeria in the current day. Nigeria is facing some of its worst unrest in years. Whether or not it has caught the attention of Western media, Oluwapelumi is keen to encourage our gaze to rest on the visage a little longer.

Why, you ask? Because it is through the eyes that one can engage the heart. And Oluwapelumi sees the people of Nigeria as the heart of the matter. We live in a time when protesting has become lethal. And despite international outrage, little or nothing is done. As is often the case, the dominant rhetoric camouflages what is really happening on the ground.

You could be forgiven for being overwhelmed. However, Oluwapelumi has set himself a task, one charted by the title poem, in which he interrogates tenderness on the West African body. Tenderness is mentioned four times across the collection and twice in the first poem. In medicine, tenderness suggests pain or discomfort when an affected area is touched. Oluwapelumi, being a medical student, would know this. Tenderness can also represent gentleness and affection. The collection is held in the tension between these two meanings of the word: the pain of the Nigerian body when touched and the gentleness of touch that it requires. Oluwapelumi is reaching for a certain heart posture that the nineteenth-century British novelist Jane Austen speaks of in her novel *Emma*: "There is no charm equal to tenderness of heart."

Oluwapelumi reorients how we look at the Nigerian body, and by proxy, the Nigerian story. In essence, these poems are portraits of Nigeria and the people of Nigeria. The portraiture mode allows Oluwapelumi to oscillate between reality, fiction, eulogy, and satire. It is a technique he adopts to direct our gaze on the martyrs, vagabonds, lost boys of the sea, and so on. Sometimes the lens is wide enough to allow him to move across time:

> Three years
> into the future, all the children in Ilé-Ifẹ̀ are lost kites
> floating away into heavenly places, and somewhere
> between fog and a clear horizon, there is a body raised
> to the sky cloaked in memory. Here, the news headline
> revamps the horror: *A missing child is another dead child.*
>
> ("Chronicle of Missing Things")

However, the lens is often narrow: "I burn my father's prayers in a heap / of hemp and marijuana. I am a vagabond / because the wind will not leave me" ("Vagabond").

Irrespective of their apertures, these poems are bound together by tenderness. They reject the idea that African identity is a monolith. How can it be, when there are between 1,500 and three thousand languages spoken on the continent? Africa is trapped in its myth, or stereotype, of being a primitive, timeless place with a generic people. Oluwapelumi's chapbook, with its acts of tenderness, undermines these backward notions. Rather than being othered, an African body can assume the protagonist role. Notice how subtly he achieves this with the following couplets:

> We are plucked from our homes
> before our tenderness ripens . . .

The air here shrivels up everything
beautiful and tender before its blooming.

("Mouthful of Cinders")

Or with these lines from "For Mama's Boys": "Our hands, like sieves, sift / every grain of tenderness."

MOUTHFUL OF CINDERS

In the name of genocide,
a father is gifted the ashes
of his burnt daughter in an urn.
His hands are diamond-heavy
with the weight of loss,
and his heart is a festering wound.
We are plucked from our homes
before our tenderness ripens.
The world, a cruel mother,
starves us of love and leaves us by the roadside
to suffer the wrath of the inflamed weather.
The air here shrivels up everything
beautiful and tender before its blooming.
In a mouth once ripe with songs,
a glossary of artillery colonizes.
The air holds her body like water, dissolving through.
I am a wanderer from the chaos,
watching from the luxury of a home.
My face boils with tears. I pray to God for rain
to wash the death, to cleanse this grief.
Inside a minaret, while praying, I eavesdrop
on a young boy as he recounts the rosaries on his takbir
for the hundredth time, waiting, praying, wishing for it all
to become history without memorabilia of scars.
I cannot tell him this is how time wears us like a skin
till our hopes age like wrinkles, or how long
we must mourn so we can sing once again someday.

VAGABOND

I burn my father's prayers in a heap
    of hemp and marijuana. I am a vagabond
because the wind will not leave me.

    The road ahead is a forbidden way
leading to a discotheque for lost boys.
    You are trying to say home, but I mistake

it for run, and so I leave. I am a homeless
    child because there is no home in me.
I am the siren song because the voice of whom

    I sing is an echo lost in the lust of silence.
The people I love are memories fleeting
    away like embers. My mother's face is a ball

of gas molded into the solid geometry
    of a cloud. I do not remember her, so the cloud
teaches me her touch. It becomes

    harder to remember my name.
The elegy of the black swan in the forest is
    for me, for things lost.

I want to return like a soul from a dream,
    but the wind tethers me. I am the wind because
I am the child with legs that knows no home.

FOR LOST BOYS AT SEA

For every lost boy at sea, the tide surfs memories of lost love.
Even the loneliness in our mute mouths creeps like a dead branch.

There used to be a song here—a marine goddess swooning.
Now, the turbulent days are upon us. Our grief is a seashell desiccating.

There is not enough pain to waft pain. Here, a boat is a sinking miracle.
There are no survivors here, only lost boys lording over flies and campfires.

Look—the white seagull across the horizon flies into morrow.
Tomorrow is an albino. We are lost by how much farther we've left home.

Shut your eyes and the distance deluges. I am swaying into the night because
the wind will not leave me. We grease the emptiness in us, and slip away . . .

FOR MAMA'S BOYS

We were boys
before the world tore our innocence
apart from our lips.

We used to chase lizards,
now our feet rummage through perils:
a serpent's venom, say oró is in the wealth
of a luxuriant garden, say orò.

This is the origin of our tremor,
the bustle of our hustle, ìbí mí je ìbí.

We seep through stables like horseflies,
where filth is home
where home is anywhere
where the night holds us guests.

On empty streets,
our hearts drown
in the liquor of silence.
It burns.

Our hands, like sieves, sift
every grain of tenderness.

Here, time is the wind's spine.
But we journey into the world with blunt blades
and pored bucklers. There are no guidelines.
Mama's boys write their own survival.

ALKEBULAN

after David Odiase

I know the taste of the brown sands
in the desert, the salt in our seas,
the venom in our veins.
I know the scent of tobacco
on my grandfather's lips
and the amala buried
under my mother's fingernails.
I know the scent of egusi
soup diffusing into the air, like smoke.
I have known this earth to be a reservoir
for souls to canoe into dead waters.
There are birds with broken wings,
and a drafty wind swarming our seas.
The indigo of our attire no longer glistens
like glass refracting against light. Our ebony
is a panther suffering albinism.
We pour liters of eucalyptus
into a calabash of palm wine
to sweeten the sourness in our mouths.
Still, nothing yields. Here,
a girl plaits waist beads around her buttocks.
The only language her mother taught her is the black alphabet
of survival. How much more chaos
will your song contort? We carry our god in our diastema—
the revolt between our mother tongue and the white's wine.
When our names are called in their language
we wear our faces in shame.
Pray we unspool like tufts from the clog

that holds us. Pray we slog over this endless road
to reach the end that follows after the beginning.

MARTYR

I will shatter: skull split, torso dismembered
into fractions of myself on the road.

The asphalt roughening
against the turbulence of my body.
My ebony skin, razed by a flaming tire.
My rosary looped around my fingers.
Heaven, heavy on my lips
like stone-cold diamond. The chars,
glittering like God's eyes at me.

A cherub leans to my lateral plane
to flaw a fissure where my blood pours out.
The flux oranges the ground with angst.
The air sits in the opulence of my empty heart.

I will stare back at the rage of the assailant's machete
and see nothing but a lance of light
spoking my martyrdom.

FRACTALS

The mind diffracts into ruptured wavelengths,
cranium fragments into ellipses of memories,

and a city built in enamel gnashes iron—
every edifice plunged into the throat of ruin,

I am becoming a limb of reality—amputated
& left to rot in the cocoon of dream-ingesting maggots.

In the dark, a cricket chirps, singeing its wings,
as it harmonizes the broken cadence of a lullaby

swooning me into rest. Somewhere, between
whole and holeness, I lie, the gap sinking into me

like an inhalation, my body a door with no door
leading to a discotheque. Everything before me

is a grave. I am a walking corpse. In the sky, a dark moon
hovers with crows clustered into a murder of feathers.

Tinctures of hope besmirch my face, my lungs turn
godless—defiled by an ennui wanderlusting

across the rooms of my body. I press on a clavicle
and a rip cord ricochets my neck off my head.

CHRONICLE OF MISSING THINGS

My mother's prayers fall back into her mouth.
A son is lost, and father's eyes quicksilver into
sheen ash. *See no evil. Hear no evil.* And a voice
traveling into the distance returns an echo lost
of its breath. My mother still beads adhans into a rosary
at the minaret, a mouth blooming thorns. Three years
into the future, all the children in Ilé-Ifẹ̀ are lost kites
floating away into heavenly places, and somewhere
between fog and a clear horizon, there is a body raised
to the sky cloaked in memory. Here, the news headline
revamps the horror: *A missing child is another dead child.*
All the elders in my hometown assemble, melting into shadows
as another child's sandals lick the ground. A crow perches
on the house, and the night pulps us into tragedies again.
The light has escaped our faces again. Woe to the road
leading nowhere. Woe to the wind severing the umbilical cord
between a mother's love and a child's tenderness. The weaning
hands now hold stillness and cradle silence in a quilted embrace.
This chronicle writes our brothers into history; tufts of tassels
flailing in the wind to become fleeces dissolving in vinegar.
My mother, at the crest of dusk, counts stars in the sky,
and somewhere, there is a son carved in the face of light.
I fold the silhouette of my brothers' panegyrics into
my mother's lips and somehow they are alive in our lips,
in every song where they aren't clothed as elegies.
Our sons are not lost. They are returning and we await
their arrival, sitting at the edge of our prayer mats.

OKÁN

There is a thin vein between èjé and eje
by which I mean even the body betrays its
oath of staying alive. In this poem, I am ogún
but an age is merely a measure of how much war
you must wear. Mother chastises my bravado
and calls me hunter's tail and I stare
as the oro slides on her lips like oró, like poison,
like taboo. A lioness teaches her sons to
be cubs, but here, Mother plucks the seeds
from our fangs and plants the gum of fear. She
says fear is safety. Courage is iku. Even
my dialect warns me, okán for courage, also
for heart, and a lacerated nymph for hoe, yet
I chose to sit with the sun confusing its dusk for
rest. Home warns us too with its transient
epithet; how ilé with a windy alteration of its
tonal oath could become ilè; a nomenclature
for grave. The truth is this, whether the ram feigns
bravery or wears a coat of fear, the slaughterman
will not stop the swoop of his swiveling saber.

ELEGY

after Danusha Laméris

I stand at arm's length from your corpse.
There is a universe between us
yawning light. Nothing sees dawn here.
Maggots, grubs, houseflies, and midges
creep out from your rib cage.
There is a hive in your throat where silence
buzzes. The soil you sleep on swelters
with soot. Dreams are an abyss—you fall in blind.
I look through your eyes and they refract the light
pouring into them like glass.
Some leave, some leaven, and some live.
You are an island where hungry crocodiles circle
in ambush. Forgive me, I could not
save you. You are a dying species.
The world burns, and soft bodies like yours
cannot survive the heat. Even water
burns here. Ask me for the ashes
and I will bring them to you. Love, your voice
like a song sifted through a sieve is nothing
but silence now, a feather falling through wind.
There is a magnolia flower growing in the soil
your blood seeped into. I see your smile
in its blossom. Its petals like your skin
sermonizing the light with colors. The darkness
has painted you into a shadow, and now
you no longer exist in the light. You eclipse.

BLACK

with a line borrowed from Warsan Shire, for David Oluwale

1.

To be born black
is to be christened death.
I am a testament

of every mass grave
called a country instead
of a cemetery.

Around us, an ambush circles:
a city of walls has been
built around our bodies.

2.

In our mouths, an anthem
becomes elegy,
mourning the leaves of memories

decaying in the forest
of our hearts. Brother, here
there is always prey.

3.

Who will walk with me
into a prayer with bridges
at the verge of collapsing?

Look! There goes a black bxy,
his body sliced in half
like an unripe pomegranate.

I have seen deaths
enough to make the human eye
a city of graves.

4.

O brother, we are blank pages:
we were born to be maimed,
brutalized, massacred, and killed.

5.

No one unnames themselves.

No one runs from their country
unless their country
is a shark's mouth.

MOTHER TONGUE

"Terrors take hold on him as waters,
a tempest stealeth him away in the night."
—Job 27:20

it is the beginning of harmattan

throw a matchstick
into the jungle
and watch it choose
what it burns.

watch it choose me.

the flowers of the neem tree
blossom new seeds
like full moons.
the Nile burns alive.

i am a wildflower in a wildfire.

carve my country's name
into the scalp of a dolomite.
its surfaces glitter
like sand ashened with lightning.

a lake swallows my English
and spits out silence
salted with my mother's dialect.

WATER

1

I am stretching from sinew to bone
to muscle the distance.

My heart is a basket of citrus
seeping through.

My flaws are fatal miracles.

A bonfire
warms my wounded bones to life.

    We share blood and our veins bleed into confluence in an oasis.
 I reach for the pier and I am clinging to absent salvation.

2

The lake is history
        a dead thing by the wharf.

Memory is a boneyard
   an ocean in arrhythmia.

I pulse through reckless waves
  the tide roughening
against my face.

3

my family drowned in the war—

the lost aborigine says—

I chew a mouthful of cinders
to rust the inferno.

At the end of the war
everything burns.

Scorched cadavers
breath burnt air.

The stories in Biafra are feared in a bloody climate.
It rains gunpowder and the air leaves marks on our skin.
It is a year of blood. The hemorrhage starts to blush.

4

O Lord,
the sea is littered with wrecked boats
and drowned corpses,

but we must cross.

Teach us how
not to drown—

ACKNOWLEDGMENTS

Many thanks to the editors of the literary magazines where some of these poems first appeared in earlier versions or under different titles.

Isele Magazine: “Mouthful with Cinders” (retitled “Mouthful of Cinders”)
A Long House: “Vagabond”
20.35 Africa: “Alkebulan”
Lucky Jefferson: “Missing” (retitled “Chronicle of Missing Things”)
Poet Lore: “Untitled” (retitled “Okán”)
Rising Phoenix Review: “For Lost Boys at Sea”
TAB Journal: “Fractals”
IHARF United and Unique Anthology: “Black”